THE LOST TRIMESTER

THE LOST TRIMESTER

Diamond Williams

This book is for me
but it's also for you.
I wanted to show you
the mess we've been through
can be part of the journey,
an unfortunate fate
where Grief and Healing
share an estate.
Where my pain and yours
share the same ink,
on pages of hurt
where our stories interlink.

You have to put a trigger warning
Before you talk miscarriage mourning
Sometimes I laugh
Sometimes I joke
Other times I hold my breathe until I choke
But mostly I just hold my tongue
When I make a post reaching for a lifeline
And social media says I violated their guidelines
By talking about some real shit I went through
Don't they know I'm trying to make a
breakthrough?
I'm trying to normalize the burden we share
As women who've lost a child
The world pretends to care but it's not their
problem to bear
So we speak on it a little
but it needs to be a lot
When half the women you know
Have their womb in knots
From the pain of pregnancy loss or stillbirth
You'd rather just ignore it because you are
uncomfortable
But what is that worth?
       Your silence is insufferable
       We won't be governable
       Let's all get vulnerable
       Because if we don't the damage for
       future generations will be irrecoverable

Make it normal
Teach it in schools
Make sure kids know it can happen to me or you
To your mom or your sister your daughter or
your wife
This conversation needs a place in everyday life
So when someone else
Goes through this pain
We can together make flowers from rain
And they won't be alone on their darkest of days
If we make it relatable they won't feel ashamed
They will feel only human
An unexpected flaw in the plans
Because that's what miscarriage is
A glitch in the matrix we'll never fully comprehend

CONTENTS

d.n. williams

CREATING YOU

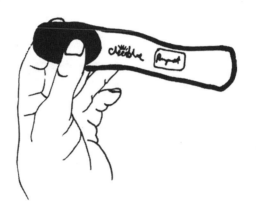

Two pink lines and my missing breath
How much time has passed since I took the test?
I don't know
But from this moment you've been fleeting
From me
You've been something scary and wonderful
All at the same time
Exhausting my mind trying to wrap it around the
thought of you
In this moment it's only us
Before I tell him
Before the world outside of these bathroom walls
Knows our secret
For a second I pause
Still admiring the proof of you in my hands
Wondering who and what you'll be
In this moment
From the first thought of you
I became your mother
In this moment
You became my baby

Less than nine months from now
I will be holding a baby in my arms
I have to say it again
To convince myself of its truth
I see you on the ultrasound
And I feel a tug
Deep in my chest
I wipe a tear from my cheek
Unaware that I was even crying
But it's you little one
Who I've waited for days on end
Its you that we have wanted for so long
Are you real?
When will I let it sink in that I will have you
Nine months from now

It is so fast
That rapid heartbeat of yours
It's faint and small
But it's there
The tiny heart on the screen made in love
By the two people that will raise you
With the same love that formed your being
A love that is loud and untamed
A love that can also be soft and tender
Which is what you too will be
My dear
A wildflower
Delicate in many ways but determined
To survive in the harshest conditions

Waking up each morning
With an immediate turning in my stomach
That I have to admit I do not enjoy
But that sick feeling reminds me
That you are there and you are alive
Thriving in my womb
This feeling will fade
I will no longer feel poor
And I'll get to nourish you until you arrive
Soon to be here in my arms
Soon to be in all of our lives
Exactly where you belong

I find this too good to be true
Not in an impossible way
More like in the way you find
A one hundred dollar bill on the ground
Looking around waiting for someone
to claim your fortune
Waiting for someone to jump out of the bushes
And tell you you've been punk'd
Inside I scream and jump
Rejoicing in the confirmation that is you
This is real
YOU are real
and you are mine

Please don't be
Too good to be true

LOVING YOU

Butterfly baby
The flutters of you
will always be wanted

I'd be lying if I said
The thought of you
didn't make my stomach do somersaults
It could be the nerves
But it could also be morning sickness
Either way
You are here
Growing slowly
Soon to be a part of my world
It takes time to adapt
But I'm adapting at the speed of light
with every breath I take breathing life into you
I'm adjusting to the wonderful thoughts
flooding my mind
Of you in your fathers arms for the first time
And your brothers kissing your cheeks
The split second of fear
after finding out about you
Is soon forgotten
as I revel in your newfound existence

As I look at my changing physique
I smile a smile
that only my soul could feel as genuine
A smile that pulls from within
Knowing that is where you will reside
Until I bring you into this world
From an
orifice whose true purpose
Is giving you life

I didn't know how to tell him
That I already loved you
That I already had a connection to you
Like a budding rose that needed the stem to
carry its weight
He doesn't know you yet but I do
I know you like I know my own breath
I've felt your presence since before I knew you were
Growing inside of me
We have the same blood
Your heart beats because of mine
And mine in turn beats for you little one
He will love you
I know he will but he will feel shock
It will take him longer than I to feel
the magnetism of your being
But when he does
From that day forward
He will be your greatest protector
Your most devout supporter
And give you the fiercest unconditional love
you will ever know

I had a feeling
That you would be a girl
I called you Capri
Picturing you as a young woman
Full of life and adventure
Beautiful and wild
Just like I used to be
Envisioning a day I would take you to Italy
Where we would spend our days shopping
and basking in the sun on the Amalfi Coast
Cupping you inside of me with my hands
I whisper
The words of the song playing on the radio
'Oh Capri, she's beauty, baby inside she's loving'

Tiny hands
Gliding gently
across my tight belly
Not knowing the full extent
Of the life growing beneath
The way they once grew

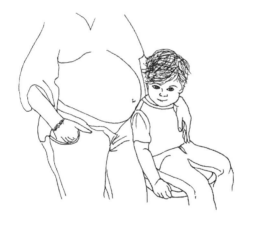

Walking along a narrow trail
On a rocky mountainside
In late spring
It's sunny and warm
But the wind is crisp
As it carries my toddlers voice
Through the air
Past my ears

Turning towards my name
I see him kneeling
On a patch of flowers
Just as he plucks one from the
Leftover snow
I notice it's the last standing
Mountain Aven
In the patch

I cradle the buds in one hand
His little hand in the other
And for the rest of the walk
I think of the Aven
How it reminds me of you

And how just as your big brother
Picks flowers for me
He will be picking flowers for you
One day too

I bought you clothes today
Something simple and sweet
Then I hung it in your closet on a
Soft velvet hanger
I look around the room and think about
Where I will rock you to sleep and feed you
Tell you stories and sing you songs
This room will be a nice place for us
To escape the world and indulge
In moments that are only ours
Like my body is now
Yours as much as it is mine
As you spend your days soundly
Growing inside

My DNA changed
The instant you began

I carried you
Just long enough
To let your little fingers
Leave permanent prints
On my heart

I remember the exact moment
Losing you
Changed me forever

Note to self:
This too shall pass
But when it does
Don't let it make you cold

LOSING YOU

I can't remember
What I had for breakfast
Or where I put my keys
I don't always remember my
Grocery list
Sometimes
I forget if I'm twenty-nine
Or thirty
But I will never forget
Every detail from the moment
I was suddenly
Half of who I was before
You died

The word miscarriage
Has society in shambles
a bitter taste on their tongue
Leaving them to ramble
On and on with empty condolences
The discomfort they feel
Deems the word inappropriate
For a casual conversation
between colleague or acquaintance
We need to do something
to make this an acceptance

It's not a taboo
It's mentally draining
You can't veto a feeling
It's physically devastating

A 'spontaneous abortion'
One out of four women
Have experienced
Ashamed so it's hidden

Day in and day out
She functions the same
Completing all the tasks ahead
She has for the day
Cramping and bleeding
Headaches and a constant needing

Feeling
to scream and cry
and hit or kick anything in sight
Because how dare she not be under control
Of her own body's ability of a child to grow
So when you look at a woman
Just keep in mind
She might be dealing with an invisible struggle
Don't be left behind

In the ways of a world stuck in the past
We need to talk about pregnancy loss
We need to be the last
Generation
to think the word miscarriage should be prohibition

Like it's a dirty word
That will make you feel nasty
That's fucking absurd

ONE-IN-FOUR WOMEN
        Get that through your head
Why should we feel alone
    Because the topic fills YOU with dread?

Just as quickly as I knew
Those pink lines meant you
I knew what the blood meant too

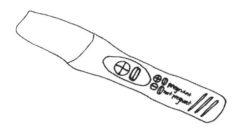

Like a knife to my abdomen
A twisting that I wish I didn't know
All too well
A wet sensation that can only mean one thing
Keeping hope alive until the morning
Where the Doctor will confirm
There will be no you
There will be no sonogram or gender reveal
There will only be the aftermath of what is left
The next two weeks
a reminder that you're gone
with each bit of you that leaves me

Cold gel on the wand
Slight pressure between
My legs
shaking
A nervous reeling
It's been weeks since I've seen you
Can't shake this feeling

Unnerving and hopeful
All at once
'Let me get the doctor'
Says the nurse in a hollow tone
This doesn't feel right
I cup my belly
My chest becomes tight

I sit there and wait for what feels like forever
I pray to any God that will listen
Please don't sever this tether

A knock at the door
and a silent entrance
The doctor finds no heartbeat
No life left at chance
Sometimes this happens
It's not your fault
His words didn't keep me
From falling apart

Or blaming myself
        On the days of deep depression

                Missing you my only obsession

He didn't deserve this
The torture of imagining
His life with three beautiful children
Them the rug being torn out from under him
Like a magic carpet that lost all of its wonder
As the words
'I'm having a miscarriage'
Slip off my lips in a new somber tone
So unfamiliar to us both
He didn't deserve the excitement
To be squandered so soon
Before we even had a chance to share it
Your father is the most incredible man
I have ever known
This man who helped me create
Your blooming life
Doesn't deserve to feel the mourning
Of the baby he never got to look in the eyes
That were so sure to be his own looking back

Sitting on the shower floor
Watching tiny water pellets
Connecting to one another before they roll
Down the tile my head rests against
As the steam fogs up the glass
As the temperature changes from hot to warm
to cold
As the water sprays the left side of my face
As it masks the tears from my eyes
that aren't mine to control anymore
While all of it washes over me from top to bottom
Taking with it the red remembrance of you
From my body
Across the white acrylic in a stream
Down the drain
With the water that takes you so swiftly
Like another little piece of my soul that
belongs to you

How do you say goodbye
To someone you loved
but never got the chance to meet?

angel baby

I sit on the cold porcelain
My legs pressed firmly against the seat
Looking down I see only what is left
I see only in red
Cradling my head in my hands
Shaking as if I no longer have control of my body
The body who made you and the body
Who couldn't keep you

I see red for days
I see red until I think I will burst from the inside
I don't want to see red anymore
You were supposed to be pink or blue
But instead you are RED
Crimson in the most volatile form
Remnants of you on my garments
so I throw them away
I cannot keep something that contained a
lifeless you
But then how can I keep me?
How can I keep this body void of your
blooming life?
The life I yearn for that felt so close to mine
How can I keep me?
This body that held you as you slowly faded away
Before there was nothing left
This body that has no control of if you stayed
How can I keep me?
Do I even want to keep me?

red red red red red red red red red *red* red <u>red</u> red
red <u>red</u> red red red *red* red red red red red red
red red red red red red red red red <u>red</u> red red
red red *red* red red red red red red red red r*ed*
red red red red red red red red red red red red
red red red red red red red *red* red red red red
red red red red red red red red red red red red
red red red red red red red red red red *red* red red
red red red red red red red red red red red red
red *red* red red red red red red red red red red
red red red red red red red red red red *red* red
red red red <u>red</u> red red red red red red red red
red red red red red red red red red red red red
red red red red red red red red red red red red
red red red red red red red red red red red <u>red</u>
red red red red red red red red red red red red
red red red red red red red red red red red red
red red *red* red red red red red red red red red
red red red red red red red red red red red red
red red red red red red red red red red red red
red <u>red</u> red red red red red red *red* red red red
red red red red red red red red *red* red red red
red red red red red red red red red red red red
red red red red red red red red red red <u>red</u> red
red red red red <u>red</u> red red red red red red red
red red red red red *red* red red red red red red
red red red red red red red red red red red red
red red red red red red red red red red red red
red red red red red red red red red red *red* red red
red red <u>red</u> red red red red red red red red red
red red red red red red red red red red *red* red
red red red *red* red red red red red red red red
red red red red red red red <u>red</u> red red *red* red red

My heart
Is like a record that's been
Scratched
Destined to skip a beat
Each time the needle
Makes its way over this part
Of my song

*Note to self:
Don't stay this bleak forever
You have to warm up eventually

GRIEVING YOU

Days go by
I feel pain
Make it stop
make it go away

Grief is a funny thing
One day you can't get out of bed
And the next
You're laughing with friends
At a concert
One day you're physically sick
And the next
You're productive and running errands
In town without a care in the world
But the funny part
Isn't really funny at all
When it can hit you like a high speed truck
At any given moment
Grief doesn't care
If you made plans or have work
Grief comes and goes
Whenever it wants

The world wasn't ready
for you
But I was

How do you tell them?
Do you make a group text?
Do you send an email,
That there won't be a next?
Do you tell them in person,
Do you give them a call?
To say over a static line
they didn't make it after all

How do you tell them
The life that you grew
Just stopped growing
There's nothing they can do
You know they loved them too

How do you look your father in the eye
And say without shame
That his grandchild has died.
How do you tell your brother that he won't be
an uncle
No more limbs on the tree

Speaking of trees
How do I tell
My grandparents about
How I'm living in hell
Trying to think of the right words to say
A soft way to tell them
no more cousins to play

How do I even go about saying
Your sibling has died
To my very own babies
How do I tell my very best friend
That her future godchild
Has come to an end

How do I sleep at night next to my husband
When he expressed how he needed me
And I told him I couldn't

How do I look myself in the mirror
When the woman looking back had her body
betray her
How will I tell every stranger on the street
The agony I'm feeling as I look at my feet
Instead of meeting their peering gaze
My mind will forever be lost in a haze

I'll be different from now on
I don't know what to do
How will I tell them,
        'It's me, not you'

With every cramp
I shudder
Knowing it's my bodies
Way of telling me
You're leaving me

Telling my mother was harder than most
Over the phone since we didn't live close
Just weeks after I gave her the news
that she'd soon have a grandchild
Pink or blue
I gave her a onesie
Wrapped as a gift
The word grandma
Written in print
After just one ring
She picks up the call
Understanding my words
Through sobs and all
She says, 'I'm so sorry baby'
Almost on demand
somehow she softens the pain
In a way only she can
It wasn't long ago
She lost a baby of her own
Now she suffers again
With her own that is grown
Because when a daughter's heart breaks
Her mothers does too
It might even be worse
Because it's breaking for two

Our two bedroom apartment
Was much too small
We knew a new house
Would be the right call

Driving around
Looking at listings
Trying to find
What we were missing

Finally, we found the one
A cozy house trimmed in blue
We made new renovations
Now all we needed was you

We got the news
Just a week before
We were set to move in
I didn't want the house anymore

All fees were paid
Now there was no going back
The truck was on its way
To help us unpack

Our first night in that house
I laid next to your empty crib
In the nursery we didn't need
Knees pressed to my ribs

Do I dare call it progress
When I think of you
and don't cry?
I want to feel happiness in its entirety
But I get swept away with a tide
Of ocean waves when I try

My apologies
For what I said
When I was grieving

**I don't know how long my body has rested in
this bed**
My figure becoming one with the mattress
Not knowing where the sheets begin and my
skin ends
I don't know the time of day
And the windows have been drawn for what
feels like
An eternity
But I like it
I want to leave my soul in the dim light of this room
Until I stop thinking of you
Until I stop blaming myself for losing you
Until I stop blaming my body for not doing what
it was made for
Or until I stop wondering what I could've done
differently to keep you safe
And I guess it's working because I don't feel much
Other than the somatic response
from my bones underneath me
The involuntary breathing I seem to be counting
Or the sips of water I force myself to take
between naps
Naps that don't seem like sleep because
I close my eyes and I dream of the life I would
have with you
Or I wake in a sweat from a nightmare my
Mind cannot shake
I don't know how long my body has been rested
in this bed
But it doesn't feel like rest at all

When my dad got remarried
I got an extra mother
It took some time
Getting used to another
But as the years went by
From child to teen
We bonded over clothes, boys
Everything in between

So when I grew up
I couldn't wait to
Surprise her with the news
About little bitty you

She was so excited
We hugged and cried
Then a week later
I had to tell her you died

We cried and hugged
But it was different this time
With no little life
Still growing inside

No one will ever understand
The grief that overcomes me
When I think of who you might have been

**Note to self:
A fervent woman
Still has frigid days

LEAVING ME

Months go by
I feel numb
All emotions have been taken
By my black thumb

To the people that love me
Some days I feel so much
I feel like my soul can't take anymore torment
before it gives up on me completely
The way theirs gave up on them when they left me
Some days I feel so little I wonder if I'll ever
feel again
The numbness creeping up on me
Like mold in an old house that someone has
forgotten
The self-pity suffocating me in silence
As I scream in my mind
While my face remains a blank page
Awaiting a story that I don't know how to write
I want to find a day or place
Where I feel normal again
But what is normal in this sea of grief?
I'm drowning and everyone is watching to see if
I'll swim
To see if I'll save myself
but for what?
To live out partially cloudy days when everyone
around me
Is experiencing sunshine
Until I swim
Until the cloud hanging over me clears
Please be patient with me
Be my life raft
Be my sunshine
Be what I cannot be for myself

Searching for a less constant emotion
Each day that passes feeling more detached
Than the last
Dazed in a state of numb I haven't known
Until now
At least thinking of you doesn't sting
Today the way it did yesterday
Maybe the pain has put a paralytic on my mind
That it needed to survive

Speaking of being paralyzed
I feel like I'm dreaming
Running running running
Trying to escape a terrible monster
But my legs don't surpass a slow walk
Screaming screaming screaming
But my lungs aren't filling with the air
I need to call out to you
Then I realize I am in fact not asleep
In a nightmare
But in a miserable reality
where I've lost you completely

Who is she?
The one who looks back at you
In the mirror
With tired eyes and an even more tired soul
With a darkness about her
That makes you wonder if there was ever any
light in her
To be found
What hurt her?
Was it the loss?
Was it the pain in her stomach reminding her of
your absence?
Or was it the questioning of your existence
inside her all along?

I want to distance myself
From this person I've become
Since losing you
She's not someone I recognize
She's not someone I want in my life
She's not who I want to be
But distancing yourself from
A whole part of you
Seems more difficult
When you see your own reflection
through a fogged mirror of sorrow

How does everything hurt
When I feel so numb inside?

He doesn't deserve me like this
For better
For worse
Those were our vows
But it feels all wrong now
There should have been some fine print
For cases like this

He doesn't deserve me like this
When the collapse of you
Unraveled me like a ball of yarn
Rolled across a hardwood floor
Forgotten under the side table

He doesn't deserve me like this
I'm sickness
He's health

He doesn't deserve me like this
Riddled with a disease
The grief has left me with
He now has to deal with illness
That coats my heart
Like fresh tar on a newly paved road

Which is ironic because if his love alone
could fix me
The cracks in the road underneath
Would already be sealed

He doesn't deserve me like this
A pessimistic woman where an optimist once stood

So full of hope and anticipation of the life we
created together inside me

He doesn't deserve me like this

He deserved me as the mother I should be
Not the bereaved person our loss had made me

I want to be me again
But I don't know how

Don't judge her right away
That woman you see in aisle 12 staring at the cereal
As if choosing the right one
is the hardest decision she's ever made
Her hair is ratted in a bundle on top of her head
And her wrinkled clothes seem to have been
chosen in the dark from a hamper somewhere
you see, she isn't struggling to choose a cereal
She's struggling with so much more
She is staring into an abyss so deep
the world around her has faded away
Because two aisles back she passed the baby
formula
She saw rows of diapers
And now her head is spinning down a rabbit hole
Swallowing her up with emotions too big to let
her escape
In fear that she might turn into a liquid puddle
completely
Her heart beating at a frequency lower than before
she bore an empty womb
So please don't judge her right away
You don't know what she's been through
When she finally looks up and grabs a box of
Cheerios
Turning toward you with a flushed look of
humiliation
After realizing she's been there far too long
Simply shoot her a smile and give her the grace
she so very much deserves

There aren't many things I dislike more
Than seeing a mom and her baby at the store
Or even a toddler
A much older child
Just the sight sends me into a spiral
But don't be mistaken
I'm not an evil person
I'm happy for the mother
Who doesn't share this burden
Of the emptiness I feel
When I see her baby reaching for her
As she steps away to stock her cart

I hate myself for feeling this way
But there is nothing I can do
In the midst of the moment
All I think of is you
I too should be able to do the mundane task
Of going to the grocery store
Without spinning out of control
A sick feeling in my core

If things went my way you'd be here by now
    I'd be chatting with that woman
    All about how
    Our babies are happy
    and close in age
    But our book stopped short
    like a rip in the page

I left me
When you left me

So how do I look for me
When there is no
finding you?

In my dreams
That's where I'll look for you
I can't sleep on my own
So I'll take a pill or two
Won't be long now
Wash it down with 100-proof
In my dreams, angel
I'll see you soon

MISSING YOU

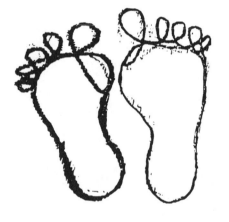

Years go by
I feel happy
I forget you for a second
Then guilt engulfs me

Everything happens for a reason
The condolences begin
No one knows what to say
The loss of a life brings the grief from the backseat
to the forefront of every conversation
But for me
it's already on my flesh
It's been there since the second you were gone
Like air to a burn
Unable to stop the pain no matter what I do
With each 'I'm sorry'
The exposed nerves vibrate across my melted skin
Raw and trying to heal on their own
With no medication to soften the agony

If our bodies
hold all of our past traumas
Mine must still be holding you

White picket fence
The dog the car
On the porch with your dad
Watching you in the yard
Play and laugh
Laugh and run
The dream I had before you'd begun
To slip away
And by the time I knew
You were already gone
Nothing left I could do
But hold onto the dreams of you
I made in my head
I'll think of them while I lay in this bed
So bound here I can't think
Of anything more
Than who you'd come to be

When will it stop
This grief I never asked for
This ache in my chest
I'll feel forever more

There it is again
That numbing feeling that leaves you
Staring at the wall
Counting the floorboards just to then
Drift back into a dream world that exists
Only to keep you alive
As the sweet little baby I always imagined
The 'you' I had thought up so many times
From the color of your eyes to the way you
would smell
So I leave my universe that never knew you
To the dream world where I have you

I have to busy myself
With other forms of devastation
In order to
Free myself
From the never ending
'What if' scenarios
Of the life you couldn't have

The life WE couldn't have

What is a world without pain?
A world without pain is you in my arms
Wrapped in soft cotton
On the front porch
While I sit with your father
And watch your brothers play in the yard
A world without pain is your fifth birthday
Where I would bake your cake
And decorate it with Barbies and candles
A world without pain is your first date
Your dad's arms over me as we wave
While you drive away after
He promised to have you home before 10
A world without pain is your wedding day
You dressed in white like an angel
As I slip on your veil
And whisper in your ear that he is
The luckiest man in the world
A world without pain is
Your first big promotion
You calling me just to say 'hi, mom'
The first time you have a real fight
And come over so I'll hold you and tell you
Everything will be alright
Your baby shower
And every milestone in between
That I get to watch
Because you are my daughter
A world without pain
Is a world where I don't dream up
Your entire life
Just to watch you slip away from me
Before I had the chance to bring you to life

I drive to the mountains
I climb towards the sun
So I can scream on top of the world
at the top of my lungs, 'what have I done?'
But I've done nothing wrong and neither have you
It's just something we as women go through

With no rhyme no reason
It just happens they say
No explanation
It just goes away

So I'll scream at the sky
Yell at the moon
Because Mother Nature took you away
From me, far too soon

Not to sound dramatic
But the turmoil that is my life
Has been swallowing me whole
Like the mouth of a whale
And I'm the sailor engulfed in the belly
Not to sound dramatic
But an asteroid has hit my heart
And left a crater the size of Jupiter
Since you went to be with the stars
Not to sound dramatic
But sometimes I sit in our chair
Next to your crib
Holding a blanket I wished contained you
While I look at the birds singing
Songs of joy out the window of your nursery
Not to sound dramatic
But my world is so dramatic
Without being able to know you

She woke up feeling alive again
She felt the warmth of the sun on her face
Through the slivers of space in the blinds
Morning stretches
Rubbing of eyelids
She slides her hand delicately across her stomach
In an effort to caress the love
She was coming to know
Then she remembered
You were gone

There are days where I feel my missing you
Slipping into the distance
And then there are days I feel like it's suffocating me
That's how I know the grief I feel in your absence
Will never be gone completely
But the better days make me long for more
like them
So I try to live for you now
Even on my bad days
Instead of allowing the hurt to consume me
I let my love for you heal me

Note to self:
I don't know if you'll feel better today
Or tomorrow or the next
But I do know you will feel better
Eventually
We've been here before
There is light on the other side of this darkness
And that's where you will feel better
in the brightness of another day that hasn't yet come
I promise you'll feel it

HEALING ME

Days go by
I feel ~~pain~~ *more like me*
  ~~Make it stop~~
  ~~Make it go away~~

What if I'm better at the dark parts?
What if I'm better at feeling the hurt
And accepting the disappointment?
More than I'm better at feeling the hope that
comes along with
The happiness that surrounds you
What if the dark is a forever thing that has swept
over the light parts of me?
What if everything I've been through has made
the light unbearable
Because of the fear that the dark will always
creep back in?
But it's just that, isn't it?
The darkness
It's a creeping shadow lurking around every corner
Waiting to take away the light that you've
gained back
after so long in a dim mindset
And now I'm tired of running down rabbit holes
of fear
I want to stop looking over my shoulder
I want to take back control
And so I shall
So maybe if I allow it I can live in both
Darkness and light
in a beautiful symphony of notes floating around
my world with ease
Maybe if I allow it
That space in between the dawn and the dusk
can be a beautiful place to reside

One day she woke up
And she felt something she hadn't felt
In a long time

She felt rested

A pulling sensation under my nail beds
From clawing my way back up
Out of the ravine I have been occupying
For so long I don't have a calendar count of the days

But the nights were even longer
Lying in the dark
Awake dreaming of a brighter world with a baby
I'll never know in my arms
A soreness in my limbs from finally pulling
myself up the sides towards the light of day
'I'll be ok' I say
To myself as I push a little further
'They need me'
I need me
Not this me
The old me before my heart couldn't take loss
anymore

One slip of my grasp and I'll be back at the bottom
But giving up now just isn't an option
Life is waiting at the edge
For me to begin again
With the loved ones
I do have
The ones that are here in the real and the now
The ones who stuck beside me
through the suffering
I don't know how

They never gave up on me
and that makes me keep scratching
My way to the surface
What is happening?
Is my chest less heavy?
Is my mind more free?
With every inch I feel more like me

So close to the peak I feel sun on my face
A warmth I remember from a far away place
In a distant past life that I long to recall
Could it be a time of bliss in my future
Is awaiting after all?

It's been 437 days
since I lost you
It's now 9:51pm
And today is the first day
It took this long for you to cross my mind

I caught myself smiling
Laughing with my husband in the kitchen
While he stood scrubbing the pile of dishes
That have accumulated over the past few days
I look at him and see a man who is quietly
Taking care of things I normally would
The laundry
The cooking
Cleaning and bathing our boys
Dressing and playing with them
All while I watch from what feels like
outside of my body
He knows I'm not me right now
He doesn't know when I will return
But he doesn't falter
He's soft when he touches me
And he gives me space
The space he knows I need to heal
And he doesn't realize that in doing
all of these things
He was the medicine
prescribed to fix me all along

Months go by
I feel ~~numb~~ *my*
~~All~~ emotions ~~have been taken~~
~~By my black thumb~~
      coming back to me...

Maybe I'll try again
Maybe I won't
Maybe I could turn to faith
Maybe I'll give up hope
Maybe I will cry myself to sleep
Maybe there are no more tears to weep
Maybe my mind will let me rest
Maybe all of this is a test
Maybe I can get a hobby
Maybe my brain will be too foggy
Maybe I'll spend some time at the gym
Maybe I'll drown my sorrows in gin
Maybe I will care what others think
Maybe I'll go out and overdrink
Maybe I can find a healthy way to cope
Maybe it's all too much and I won't
Maybe life is too hard to do
Maybe I'll start living my life for you
Maybe you will be my reason
Maybe there's an end to my grieving season
Maybe you'll look down from your cloud
Maybe it's time I make you proud

Maybe, starting now, I'll do whatever I want

If your body can conceive
She can do incredible things
If your body can carry
She's an angel with wings
If that same body can't finish the task
Don't count her out just yet
See, what she's done this far
She is truly a work of art

Just because she isn't perfect
doesn't mean she doesn't carry the burden
Of the pain and the suffering
you're feeling at her hands
Your body is sorry
Give her another chance
To redeem herself in the midst of the destruction
Every city is worthy of new construction

Let her show you she can heal and grow
New love
New life
Seeds bud after snow

See, after the frost has bitten and bruised
the earth becomes anew
Soft and supple waiting for flower
Your body too holds the same power

Give her a chance and she'll prove you wrong
She's wanted you to succeed all along
Whether that be physical with new life to carry
Or if that doesn't work just give it time,
Her mental load will never weary

She'll hold it down until you recover
She knows you need time too
To find in yourself a way to rediscover

I asked my reflection a question today
How did you get so strong?
She smiled a soft smile but gave no answer
I'll ask again
I say in a bold tone
Demanding an answer from the new woman
before me
How did you get so strong?
This time she keeps her smile and asked back
How did WE get so strong?

What if
I didn't need to find you after all
What if
you've been here all along

I had a conversation today
With two old friends of mine
One of them was with my Heart
Who pleaded with me to understand
why she felt the way she did
I told her I didn't blame her
And that things have been hard on us lately
That's when my Mind joined us saying,
Think about that for a second
You're apologizing for feeling sad
When sad is just a trick you play on yourself
I asked what she meant and she explains
You can only be sad if you let it consume you
My Heart agrees and says it makes her tired anyway
Then and there
Me, myself, and I
Made a pack to pick up the pieces of our
Tired soul
Put them back together
And feel the happiness
We've been craving for so long

I felt lost when I lost you
So I went looking for ways to stay connected to you
I felt you as beauty so I looked for you in
beautiful things
I started painting again and took walks downtown
Went to record shops and bookstores
On hikes alone and slept in on Sundays
Ate ice cream from the carton and went to dinner
with friends
I watched chick flicks that made me laugh until
I cried
I really just did anything to occupy my mind as
time passed
And in the midst of trying to find a connection to you
I found me instead

I'm in a bluebonnet field
It's a sunny day
The wind is blowing
Not a cloud in the way
I paint a scene in my mind
With you in a sundress
A bow in your hair
Golden curls a mess
Your brothers around you
'Don't pick them' I say
You shoot me a grin
Then do it anyway
For a moment
It almost feels real
No tears when it's over
It's time to heal

You lived for me
Now I'll live for you

Whoever you are
Wherever you are
I hope you know how
Proud I was of you
From your very first
Heartbeat

Whoever you are
Wherever you are
I hope you're proud
Of me too

Note to self:
You can be happy and grieving
At the same time
It's called growth

Thank you for making me your Mother
Though it brought me grief
I'm glad I carried you
No matter how brief

If you were looking for comfort
When you turned these pages
Read these words
And felt my pain
I hope you now find it in knowing
You are not not alone.

Woman to Woman
Bereaved to Bereaved
Mother to Mother

I understand your pain
I sympathize with your journey

Thank you for being part of mine.

Years go by
I feel happy
I forget you for a ~~second~~ *while*
~~Then~~ guilt ~~engulfs me~~
      doesn't control me
      anymore

normalize

[nawr-muh-lahyz]

verb (used with object), **nor·mal·ized, nor·mal·iz·ing.**

1. to make normal

2. to cause (something previously considered abnormal or unacceptable) to be treated as normal:

If we all talk openly about miscarriage we can normalize an otherwise taboo subject.

ACKNOWLEDGEMENTS

I want to thank my husband for his endless support, my children for their patience in me at my worst, my family for believing in me, my high school English teacher who renewed my love for literature, my friends who never stopped caring for me when I was hard to love, and everyone who supported me through my own emotional hardships.

To my babies I never got to hold, though it was an unfortunate fate, thank you for being my reason I was able to write these words. To all the women who share the same experience of loss, thank you for being my reason to share them with the world.

- d

Derek,

I know you loved them too. I'm sorry for the pain you had to endure times two. I will always be so grateful you never gave up on me at my worst and I'm so lucky to have you because everyday with you are days at their best.

To my children,

Jax, thank you for saving me from myself and for making me a mother.

Carson, thank you for saving me the second time I needed saving and for bringing much needed adventure into our lives.

Juliette, baby girl, thank you for saving me for the third time and for completing our family.

When I say you saved me, I mean it with everything in my being. I truly wouldn't be here without the three of you. You are my everyday reasons for living.

I love you endlessly,
Mom

About the Author

Diamond Williams is a mother turned poet from a small town in Texas. Growing up she envisioned her dream life in a big city, never knowing exactly where that might be. Moving to Austin at a young age, she pulled her creativity from the city she considered  home. This is where she came into her own and started her family before fulfilling her nomadic lifestyle dreams by moving to places like Atlanta, Knoxville, Denver, DFW, and Huntsville.

Williams started writing poetry early in life as a silent emotional outlet and began the poems featured in this book after her first miscarriage in 2018, continuing to write through each pregnancy and loss that followed. After years of writing in the privacy of her own journals, she realized that an open dialogue is what she wanted to contribute to the world through her written words.

The Lost Trimester *is her debut poetry collection.*

Latham Lit Publishing
Cover and Illustrations by Diamond Williams
Editor: Sarah Durkee
Editor: Whisper Hitt

ISBN: 979-8-218-34385-9

ATTENTION: SCHOOLS AND BUSINESSES
Diamond Williams books are available at
quantity discounts with bulk purchase for
educational, business, or sales promotional use.
For information, please e-mail
dnwilliamspoetry@gmail.com

Made in the USA
Columbia, SC
25 January 2024

30222366R00090